First published in October 1992.
Created and produced for Ediciones B, S.A.
by o3 BCN Packagers.
Text: Albert Delmar
Translation: Audrey Lopes
Illustrations: F. Salvà

© 1992, Ediciones B, S.A.
Rocafort, 104   08015 Barcelona (Spain)

ISBN: 84 - 406 - 3118 - 9
Depósito legal: CO 1027 - 1992
Printed and bound in Spain

Cover:
Self-portrait (1815)
Oil on canvas, 20.4x18.4 inches
Museo de Bellas Artes de San Fernando, Madrid.

U.S. & Canada Sole Importer/ Distributor
Trans-National Trade Development Corporation
New York City
Toll Free: (800) 592-2209
Telephone: (212) 922-0450
Fax: (212) 922-0462

Printed by Graficromo, S.A.
Córdoba (Spain)

GOYA

I still learn

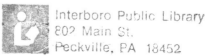

6

The story of Goya.

Francisco de Goya y Lucientes was born on March 30th, 1746 in Fuendetodos, a small village near Zaragoza.

His family belonged to the lesser nobility. However, they were very poor and lived in misery during Goya's infancy and childhood.

Goya lived during the period of the Declaration of Independence of the United States and of the French Revolution. In some countries, there were very important economic, political and social changes during this time period.

Meanwhile, in Spain, the great nobility, who had all of the money and power, lived without concern for the progress of the society surrounding them. Spain was a backward and ruined country, in which almost everyone lived in poverty. At the age of 5, Goya moved with his family to Zaragoza where, seven or eight years later, he began to work as an apprentice in the studio of the painter José Luzán. There he received traditional training, copying works by other artists and drawing dummies or live models.

They say that the first assignment his master gave him was to paint the front of a closet.

At the age of 29 he married the sister of the painter Bayeu, his second master. This marriage would be useful to him because his brother-in-law had good relations with the Court in Madrid. Thanks to this, he quickly got a job as a designer at the Royal Tapestry Factory. The Court liked his work a lot and many nobles, enthusiastic about his paintings, ordered portraits.

However, as the number of assignments increased, Goya grew tired of always painting the nice side of life.

At the beginning of his career, Goya worked at the Court of Carlos III, a king who made many necessary reforms in the country. Goya had great esteem for him.

He was succeeded by his son Carlos IV, a man who, according to his own father, was not very smart. The new king pursued and imprisoned those who wanted to modernize the country. Although Goya did not agree with his ideas, he still continued to paint for him.

In 1792 he decided to break his ties with the Court and he went to Andalucia. Once in Seville, during the winter of that year, he got very sick and became deaf.

From that moment on, his personality and his work underwent an important change. One example is the series of engravings entitled *Whims*, which he began to publish in 1799. In these engravings Goya criticizes the society in which he lives. Shortly after its publication, however, in a perfumery located in the same building where he lived, Goya removed it from circulation, perhaps out of fear of some kind of retaliation.

The Ragdoll

This is one of 63 sketches that Goya created for the Royal Tapestry Factory between 1774 and 1790.

Through Goya's work, we can find out what Spain was like at that time. Throughout his life he painted Spanish people and their customs - work, play, bullfighting... He also reflected the most important historical events, such as the War of Independence against Napoleon's powerful army (1808-1814). Most of all, Goya brought out the cruelty and the horror of its consequences.

The Ragdoll (1791-1792)
Oil on canvas, 106.8x64 inches
Museo del Prado, Madrid.

These sketches or "cartoons" were made to be copied in the form of tapestries. They were Goya's first official assignment. Bright sky, a spring-like atmosphere, cheerful colors... Recently settled in Madrid, the artist was happy and content.

All of the sketches Goya painted represented pleasant folk scenes. In this one we see four young women who are having a good time tossing a ragdoll, a human figure made of rags and stuffed with hay, up into the air with a blanket.

13

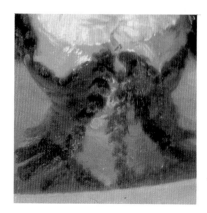

Headdresses, scarves covering their shoulders, tight waists, long, wide skirts with aprons, white stockings, light shoes with buckles… that was the fashion then!

14

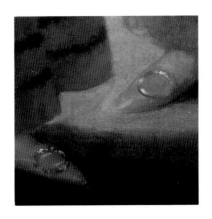

In this picture, besides showing us their game, Goya also wanted to tell us that, in his opinion, women treat men as if they were dolls!

The family of Carlos IV

This picture, painted by Goya in 1800, is an authentic masterpiece of the art of portraits.

A year before painting it, Goya had been appointed chief painter of the kingdom. He was very happy about the nomination - it meant a secure job and a good salary. That was very important for someone who had lived in misery during his childhood.

Although this is an official portrait, Goya manages to show us the real personalities behind their faces. He painted them just as he saw them, without hiding any of their defects.

The family of Carlos IV (1800)
Oil on canvas, 112x134.4 inches
Museo del Prado, Madrid.

Goya himself appears in the picture, near the royal family, but without forming part of the scene. He painted himself in the shadow, with a distant look, as though a spectator.

The young man dressed in blue in the foreground and to our left is Prince Fernando.

Queen Maria Luisa stands out in the center of the picture. She is wearing a luxurious dress and all kinds of jewels.

Goya portrays her as an older woman, with a dominant but non aristocratic look. She and her "favorite" Godoy were the ones who really were in charge of the Court. Despite this, the queen was very satisfied with Goya's work.

Goya took the liberty of painting as he pleased, since the king and queen and the nobility were great admirers of his work. Everyone, including Goya himself, was convinced that no other painter with so much talent existed.

19

King Carlos IV, a good natured man, and they say, a bit stupid, was not the person who made the decisions at the palace; and that is exactly how Goya portrays him. His distracted expression contrast with his suit full of medals.

20

The child who appears holding the queen's hand is Antonio Pascual. Encased in his glittering suit, he looks as though he is a little scared. Goya loved children, and portrayed them more affectiontely then he did adults.

The milkmaid

This was Goya's last great painting. He painted it at the age of 79, already living in France.

With Fernando VII's rise to the throne, Goya's situation at the Spanish Court grew more and more difficult. He even had to live in hiding at a friend's house for three months.

In 1824 he finally obtained authorization to move to France. After a stay in Paris, he settled permanently in Bordeaux.

He stayed there for the rest of his life. Despite his old age and poor health, he continued to work forcefully, painting, drawing or trying out new engraving techniques. He always had new projects in his imagination.

The milkmaid of Bordeaux (1824)
Oil on canvas, 29.6x27.2 inches
Museo del Prado, Madrid

In this beautiful portrait we can see that Goya painted with great freedom, without having to make corrections. It did not matter to him that his work was totally different than what was in fashion at the time.

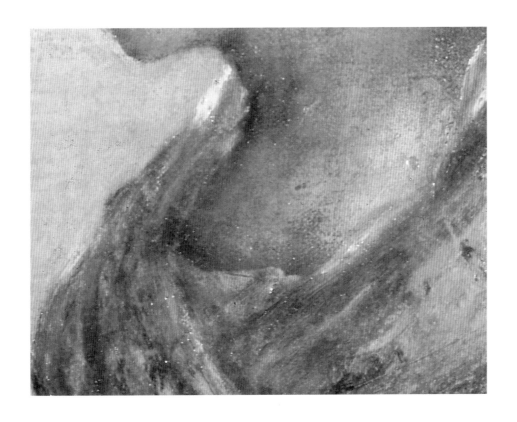

Goya liked this painting. In it, he went back to using the colors of his youth. His innovative style - the colors, the way of applying the brush… had a large influence in his paintings from that time on.

Engraving (etching)
No. 1 of the *Tauromachy* series.

26

In 1819 Goya once again fell ill and was on the verge of death. He could hardly stand up when he began his famous *Black Paintings* - witches, giants and other strange creatures, on the walls of his house. They were terrifying - like real nightmares.

The new King of Spain, Fernando VII, did not have a good relationship with Goya, who had collaborated with his enemies - the liberals. Once he even said that the painter deserved to be hung!

At the age of 77, tired of his country and discontent with is rulers, Goya left for France with the excuse that it would be better for his health. There he kept working tirelessly, never resting.

Just before dying, he wrote a letter to an old friend. In it he admitted that he could hardly see anymore and that his hands were no longer steady; that he could work only because he had one strength left - his will-power.

During that last period he created a series of lithographs, an engraving technique that had only recently been invented. One of them represented a heavy, bearded old man walking on crutches. With the title of this painting, Goya wanted to tell us how he felt - *I still learn*.

Self-portrait (1793-1795) (?)
Oil on canvas, 16.8x11.2 inches
Museo de Bellas Artes de San Fernando, Madrid.

The dressed maja (1800-1803) (?)
Oil on canvas, 38x76 inches
Museo del Prado, Madrid.

Felipe IV (1655-1660)
Oil on canvas, 25.6x21.4 inches
National Gallery, London

Francisco de Goya y Lucientes

1746 Born on March 30th in Fuendetodos, Zaragoza.

1750 He studies at the Escuelas Pías in Zaragoza.

1760 He begins an apprenticeship at the studio of the Zaragozan artist José Luzán.

1763 He goes to Madrid to work with the Bayeu brothers.

1770 He travels to Italy.

1771 Back in Spain, he receives his first assignment - decorating the vault of one of the chapels of the Pilar cathedral in Zaragoza.

1773 He marries Josefina Bayeu.

1774 He paints the frescos of the Cartuja Aula Dei in Zaragoza.

1775 He moves to Madrid. His first son, Eusebio Ramón, is born.

1777 His second son Vicente Anastasio is born.

1780 He is unanimously elected member of the Royal Academy of Fine Arts of San Fernando. He paints *Christ on the cross*. He receives the assignment of decorating the vaults of the Pilar Cathedral in Zaragoza. His third son Francisco de Paula is born.

1781 He receives the assignment from Carlos III to paint *San Bernardino of Siena praying before Alfonso V of Aragón* for the church of San Francisco el Grande, in Madrid.

1784 Under the patronage of Prince Luís of Borbon, he spends a long time in Arenas de San Pedro, where he paints *The family*. He paints four large canvases for the Calatrava School in Salamanca. His fourth son Francisco Javier is born.

1786 He is appointed the king's painter.

1787 King Carlos III gives him the assignment of three paintings for the church of the Convent de Santa Ana, in Valladolid.

1789 He is named Carlos IV's chamber painter. He paints several portraits of him.

1790 He is elected member of the Royal Academy of San Carlos, in Valencia.

1792 He falls seriously ill in Seville and becomes deaf.

1794 He paints the first portrait of the Duchess of Alba.

May 3rd shooting (1814)
Oil on canvas, 90.4x138 cm
Museo del Prado, Madrid.

Two old men eating (1819)
Mural to canvas, 21.2x34 inches
Museo del Prado, Madrid.

1795 He is Art Director of the Royal Academy of San Fernando.
1798 He paints portraits of Jovellanos, Saavedra, general Urrutia and F. Guillemardet. He begins the frescos of San Antonio de la Florida in Madrid. He works on the series of 80 etchings *Whims*.
1800 He paints the portrait of the Countess of Chinchón. He begins the portrait of Carlos IV's family.
1808 He paints the portrait of Fernando VII on horseback.
1810-14 He creates part of *Disasters of War* as a result of the War of Independence. He immortalizes the tragic consequences of May 2nd and 3rd in his paintings. He is called upon to testify before the Inquisition. He paints *The naked maja* and *The dressed maja*. He begins work on the 33 etchings of *Tauromachy*.
1816 He begins the *Nonsense* engravings.
1819 He paints the *Last Communion of San José of Calasanz* and *Farm prayer*.
1820-23 He creates the second part of *Disasters of War*.
1824 He goes to Paris and Bordeaux with the intention to expatriate. He paints many portraits.
1825 The printer Gaulan publishes four lithographs of *The bulls of Bordeaux* in Bordeaux
1828 Goya dies at the age of 82 on April 16th in Bordeaux, France.

Goya's works are principally located in:
Museo del Prado, Madrid, Spain.
Museum of Fine Arts, Boston, Massachusetts, U.S.A.
National Gallery, London, England.
Musée du Louvre, Paris, France.
National Gallery, Washington, D.C., U.S.A.
Metropolitan Museum of Art, New York, New York, U.S.A.

29

Bullfight (1825)
Oil on canvas, 17.6x22.8 cm
Museo del Prado, Madrid.